The Wonderful World of Honeybees

Written and illustrated by

Kiora Slate

Paperback: 978-1-7375225-4-6
Hardcover: 978-1-7375225-3-9
Ebook: 978-1-7375225-5-3

First Edition

Published by Kiora Slate
www.kioraslate.com

Inside an old tree, a beehive houses a family of honeybees. The worker bees fly in and out. They are always very busy.

They build the comb
that makes up the hive.

They guard the hive and
protect it from danger
by only letting in other
family members.

They fly from flower to flower, collecting sweet pollen and golden nectar to bring back to the hive.

The nectar is made into yummy honey. The pollen is made into healthy bee bread. This becomes food for the bees.

Baby bees are called brood. They look very different from adult bees. They do not have wings, antennae, or stripes yet.

When they are first born,
they are fed a special food
called royal jelly.

When they get bigger,
they are given honey and
bee bread. They eat this
their whole life.

Soon their cell is sealed
with hard wax, and they
sleep for a very long time...

...and when they wake up, they come out as a grown up bee, with shiny wings, long antennae, and dark stripes.

Boy bees are called drones. They are bigger than worker bees, but not as big as the queen.

Unlike other bees, drones
do not have stingers.

They have one job, and that is to be a loving companion to the queen.

The queen bee rules the hive. She is the most important bee, and she must be cared for and protected.

She is the mom to every bee in the hive. They work very hard to show their love for her.

They feed her royal
jelly, her favorite food.

They protect her and keep her safe from danger. She is guarded at all times by her worker bees.

They groom her and keep her clean. She must stay clean and healthy to rule the hive.

Everywhere she goes...

Every bee is important to the honeybee family. They return to the hive every night for much needed rest. Tomorrow is another busy bee day!

The End

www.ingramcontent.com/pod-product-compliance
Lightning Source LLC
Chambersburg PA
CBHW042351030426

42336CB00025B/3440